MY LITTLE BOOK OF BIG FREEDOMS

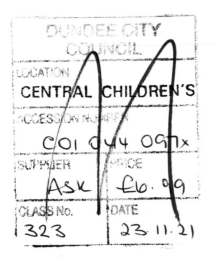

MY LITTLE BOOK OF BIG FREEDOMS

The Human Rights Act in Pictures

ILLUSTRATED BY CHRIS RIDDELL

Buster Books

in association with Amnesty International UK

I WANT TO DRAW EVERY DAY AND PROMOTE DRAWING FOR ALL -

Chris Riddell.

We all want a good life, to have fun, to be safe and happy and fulfilled.

For this to happen we need to look after each other.

In this book there are sixteen different freedoms that help look after us. They are truly wonderful, precious things.

These freedoms were created to protect us, forever.

We need to stand up for them and look after them just as they look after us.

I've drawn some pictures for you. Each of them shows one of our freedoms. I hope you like them.

Chris Riddell.

We all have the right to life.

Nobody has the right to hurt or torture us.

Nobody has the right to make us a slave - We cannot make anyone else a slave or force them to work for us.

No one has the right to lock us up without a good reason. They have to tell us that reason and let us say why we should be set free.

If we are put on trial we must be treated fairly. Nobody can blame us for doing something bad until it is proved. The people who try us must not let anyone else tell them what to do.

You can't be punished for doing something wrong if there was no law against it when you did it.

FAMILY

We have the right to live
with our family and live our
lives in the way we choose.
The government shouldn't
spy on us.

We all have the right to think or believe in whatever we like, to have a religion and to show it.

THOUGHT

We all have the right to the information we need to make up our own minds. We have the right to say what we think and share ideas with other people.

We all have the right to spend time with other people and get together to look after each other.

Every grown-up has the right to marry and have a family if they want to.

We all have the same rights.
No one can take them away
or give us different ones because
of who we are, or because we
are different from them.

Everybody has the right
to own and share things.
Nobody should take our
things away without a
good reason.

KNOWLEDGE

We all have the right to learn.

We all have the right to take part in running our country. Every grown-up should be allowed to say who they want to be their leader.

No one is allowed to Kill us,
even if we did something
very bad.

Why this little book is important

The pictures in this little book are about human rights. Human rights are special rules that belong to all of us, and look after us all. We may not have our own lion to guard our freedom, or Pegasus to wrap its wings around us, but here in the UK a special law called the Human Rights Act was passed in 1998 to look after all of us, children and grown-ups, just because we are human. This little book shows us why our human rights are so important. They help to keep us safe. Every day.

Fun activities and downloadable resources

Whether you're a child, a parent or a teacher you'll find lots of fun activities to download at amnesty.org.uk/fiction-resources

We have simplified the words of the Human Rights Act in this little book. You can find out more and see the full list at amnesty.org.uk/humanrightsact

You can find more Amnesty titles about freedom at amnesty.org.uk/books and buy them through all good bookshops and at amnestyshop.org.uk

First published in hardback in Great Britain in 2017 by Buster Books,
an imprint of Michael O'Mara Books Limited, 9 Lion Yard, Tremadoc Road, London SW4 7NQ
This paperback edition first published in 2021

 www.mombooks.com/buster ⓕ Buster Books 𝕏 @BusterBooks 📷 @buster_books

The material in this book was originally published in paperback in 2015 by Amnesty International UK

My Little Book of Big Freedoms © Amnesty International UK 2017, 2021
Illustrations © Chris Riddell 2017, 2021
The simplified version of the Human Rights Act © Amnesty International UK
Published by Buster Books in association with Amnesty International UK

A CIP catalogue record for this book is available from the British Library.

ISBN: 978-1-78055-792-2

1 3 5 7 9 10 8 6 4 2

This book was printed in April 2021 by Leo Paper Products Ltd,
Heshan Astros Printing Limited, Xuantan Temple Industrial Zone,
Gulao Town, Heshan City, Guangdong Province, China.